Anonymous

Certificate of Incorporation

Anonymous

Certificate of Incorporation

ISBN/EAN: 9783337419370

Printed in Europe, USA, Canada, Australia, Japan

Cover: Foto ©Suzi / pixelio.de

More available books at **www.hansebooks.com**

CERTIFICATE OF INCORPORATION,

CONSTITUTION AND BY-LAWS

OF THE

BUFFALO HISTORICAL SOCIETY

WITH THE AMENDMENTS TO 1875.

TO WHICH ARE ADDED

AN ACCOUNT OF ITS ORGANIZATION, A LIST OF ITS OFFICERS,
COMMITTEES AND MEMBERS, AND A BRIEF STATEMENT
OF ITS COLLECTIONS AND TRANSACTIONS.

———•••———

INCORPORATED JANUARY, 1863.

———•••———

BUFFALO:

THE COURIER COMPANY, PRINTERS.

Office of the Daily Courier, 197 Main Street.

1875.

INTRODUCTION.

On the twenty-fourth day of March, 1862, the following notice appeared in the daily papers of the City of Buffalo :

BUFFALO HISTORICAL SOCIETY.

A meeting of those of our citizens disposed to establish a Historical Society for the County of Erie, is requested at the Law Office of Messrs. Marshall & Harvey, No. 330 Main St., up stairs, on Tuesday next, 25th inst., at 7 o'clock, P. M.

GEO. R. BABCOCK,	JOHN C. LORD, D. D.
HENRY W. ROGERS,	O. H. MARSHALL,
LEWIS F. ALLEN,	WALTER CLARKE, D. D.
WILLIAM DORSHEIMER.	

In pursuance of said notice, a meeting was held at the time and place designated therein, at which the following citizens, among others, were present : Geo. W. Clinton, Henry W. Rogers, Geo. R. Babcock, Oliver G. Steele, Lewis F. Allen, O. H. Marshall, James P. White, Walter Clarke, Henry Lovejoy, William Dorsheimer, Albert L. Baker, Joseph Warren, David F. Day, Edward S. Rich, John Howcutt, and Chas. Winne.

Lewis F. Allen was appointed Chairman, and O. H. Marshall Secretary. After some discussion and interchange of views, on motion of Henry W. Rogers, the following resolution was unanimously adopted :

Resolved, That it is expedient to organize a Historical Society for the City of Buffalo and County of Erie, and that the Chairman appoint a Committee of seven to report a plan of organization.

Messrs. O. H. Marshall, Rev. Dr. Hosmer, Rev. Dr. Clarke, William Dorsheimer, James P. White, Geo. R. Babcock, and Geo. W. Clinton, were appointed such Committee.

The Committee met on the eighth day of April, 1862, and the draft of a Constitution and By-Laws was agreed to, and directed to be reported at a meeting of citizens to be held at the rooms of the Medical Association, No. 7, North Division street, on the fifteenth day of April, 1862.

At the time and place specified, and in pursuance of a general notice in the daily papers, a highly respectable number of citizens assembled, and organized, by the appointment of the Hon. Millard Fillmore as Chairman, and O. H. Marshall as Secretary.

Mr. Marshall, as Chairman of the Committee, submitted the Constitution and By-Laws prepared by the Committee, and the same were unanimously adopted. The documents were ordered to be engrossed for the signatures of all such citizens as should desire to become members.

A meeting for the election of officers was held on the twentieth day of May, 1862, at the rooms of the Medical Association, at which the following persons were elected as officers of the Society for the first year.

Hon. Millard Fillmore, ... *President.*
Hon. Lewis F. Allen, ... *Vice-President.*

COUNCILLORS.

George R. Babcock,	Nathan K. Hall,	George W. Hosmer,
George W. Clinton,	Henry W. Rogers,	O. H. Marshall,
Walter Clarke,	William Shelton,	William Dorsheimer.

At a meeting of the Board of Managers, held May 13, 1862, Charles D. Norton was appointed Recording Secretary and Treasurer, and Guy H. Salisbury Corresponding Secretary and Librarian.

On the tenth day of January, 1863, the Society was duly incorporated under the laws of the State of New York, under the name of "The Buffalo Historical Society," and the following certificate thereof was filed in the office of the Secretary of State.

CERTIFICATE OF INCORPORATION.

———— •◆•• ————

WE, the undersigned citizens and residents of the City of Buffalo, within the State of New York, of the full age of twenty-one years and upwards, and citizens of the United States, do, pursuant to the statute in such case made and provided, hereby associate ourselves together, and form a Corporation, or Society, for Historical purposes.

The name or title by which such Society or Corporation shall be known in law, is "THE BUFFALO HISTORICAL SOCIETY." The particular business and object of such Society and its general design is, to discover, procure, and preserve whatever may relate to the History of Western New York in general, and the City of Buffalo in particular, and to gather statistics of the commerce, manufactures, and business of the Lake region, and those portions of the West that are intimately connected with the interests of Buffalo.

The Officers of such Society shall be a President, a Vice-President, a Recording Secretary, and a Corresponding Secretary and Librarian, Treasurer, and nine Councillors, who, together, shall constitute the Board of Managers of said Society. The number of Managers of said Society, as aforesaid, shall be fourteen, and their names for the first year of its existence, are as follows:

MILLARD FILLMORE, ...	*President.*
LEWIS F. ALLEN, ...	*Vice-President.*
CHARLES D. NORTON, ...	*Recording Secretary.*
GUY H. SALISBURY, ...	*Cor. Sec'y and Librarian.*
OLIVER G. STEELE, ...	*Treasurer.*

COUNCILLORS.

GEORGE R. BABCOCK,	WALTER CLARKE,	NATHAN K. HALL,
WILLIAM DORSHEIMER,	ORSAMUS H. MARSHALL,	GEORGE W. CLINTON,
WILLIAM SHELTON.	HENRY W. ROGERS,	GEORGE W. HOSMER.

The principal office and place of business of such Society shall be located at said City of Buffalo in the County of Erie.

We, the undersigned members, officers, and managers of such Society, do hereby certify the matters above stated, to the end that we, our associates and successors, may, pursuant to the statute of the State aforesaid, in such case made and provided, be a body politic and corporate, by the name above stated, and in witness whereof, we have severally hereunto subscribed our names, the thirty-first day of December, 1862.

G. W. CLINTON,
ASHER P. NICHOLS,
WM. DORSHEIMER,
OLIVER G. STEELE,
HENRY W. ROGERS,

[Stamp. 10 cents.]

MILLARD FILLMORE,
LEWIS F. ALLEN,
GUY H. SALISBURY,
W. A. BIRD,
GEO. R. BABCOCK,
O. H. MARSHALL,
JOHN B. SKINNER,
HENRY DAW.

COUNTY OF ERIE, }
CITY OF BUFFALO, } ss.

On this sixth day of January, 1863, personally appeared before me, George W. Clinton, Asher P. Nichols, William Dorsheimer, Millard Fillmore, Lewis F. Allen, Guy H. Salisbury, Oliver G. Steele, William A. Bird, Henry W. Rogers, George R. Babcock, Orsamus H. Marshall, John B. Skinner, and Henry Daw, severally known to me to be the persons described in, and who executed the above instrument, and they severally acknowledged the execution of the same.

[Stamp. 10 cents.]

M. P. FILLMORE,
Commissioner of Deeds
For the City of Buffalo.

The undersigned, one of the Justices of the Supreme Court for the Eighth Judicial District of the State of New York, hereby consents to, and approves of the filing of the annexed certificate, for the incorporation of the Buffalo Historical Society.

Dated January 8, 1863.   R. P. MARVIN.

Filed in the office of the Secretary of State, of the State of New York, and in the office of the Clerk of the County of Erie, January 10, 1863.

CONSTITUTION.

——— •❡• ———

1. This Society shall be called "THE BUFFALO HISTORICAL SOCIETY."

2. The general object of the Society shall be, to discover, procure and preserve whatever may relate to the history of Western New York in general, and the City of Buffalo in particular, and to gather statistics of the commerce, manufactures and business of the lake region, and those portions of the West that are intimately connected with the business of Buffalo.

3. The Society shall consist of resident, corresponding and honorary members, who shall be elected by a majority of ballots; and of life members, as hereinafter provided. Resident members shall consist of persons residing in the City of Buffalo, *or County of Erie ;** corresponding and honorary members, of persons residing elsewhere.

4. The officers of the Society shall consist of a President, a Vice-President, a Recording Secretary, a Corresponding Secretary and Librarian, a Treasurer, and nine Councillors, who shall be elected annually, on the second Tuesday of January in each year, by a majority of ballots, and who shall constitute the Board of Managers of the Society.

5. None but resident and life members shall be eligible to office or qualified to vote.

6. Resident members shall pay an admission fee of five dollars, and also an annual due of five dollars, which shall be paid on or before the first day of November in each calendar year, after that in which they shall have been elected. The election of a resident member shall confer no privilege of membership, until his admission fee shall be paid. The payment of the annual dues shall be a condition of continued membership, and any member neglecting to pay

---

* "*Or County of Erie*," stricken out by amendment, June 8, 1869.

his annual due before the first day of January next after it becomes payable, shall thereby forfeit all his privileges of membership. *Clergy-men who are now, or who may hereafter become resident members of the Society, shall be exempt from the payment of initiation fees, or annual dues.**

The Board of Managers may authorize the Treasurer in his discretion, to receive the annual dues for any one or more years, without requiring the payment of all arrearages, and the payment of such annual dues for any one year or years, shall entitle such member to all the privileges of membership for the year or years for which such annual dues shall be so paid. †

7. The payment of fifty dollars, at one time, for that purpose, shall constitute a life member, exempt from all annual dues.

8. The Society shall meet monthly, on the second Tuesday in every month. The President, or, in his absence, the Vice-President, or either of the Secretaries, may direct the call of a special meeting in such manner as the By-Laws shall provide.

9. Those members who shall attend at any meeting of the Society shall constitute a quorum for the transaction of business.

10. All officers shall continue in office until their successors are elected or appointed. Their duties, when not herein defined, may be prescribed by the By-Laws. All vacancies in office may be filled for the unexpired term, at any regular meeting of the Society.

11. This Constitution may be amended from time to time by a majority vote of the members present at a regular meeting, provided notice of the proposed amendments be given at least four weeks previous to a final vote thereon.

---

* The words in italics added by amendment, February 15, 1871.

† The last clause in italics added by amendment, April 8, 1873.

BY-LAWS.

1. The meetings of this Society shall be held at the rooms of the Society, or at such other place as the President may appoint, and at such hour as shall be designated by the Secretary in the notice of the meeting.

2. The Recording or Corresponding Secretary shall give notice of each meeting by previous publication of the same in one or more of the daily papers of the city.

3. Any meeting may be adjourned to such time as a majority of the members present shall determine.

4. The President shall preside at all the meetings of the Society, regulate its proceedings, preserve order and decorum, and have a casting vote. He shall also be the Chairman of the Board of Managers.

5. The Vice-President shall discharge all the duties of the President in case of his absence.

6. The Recording Secretary shall have the custody of the Constitution, By-Laws, and Records of the Society. He shall give due notice of all its meetings, and keep a record of the same. He shall be the Secretary of the Board of Managers, and keep a record of its proceedings.

7. The Corresponding Secretary shall have the custody of all letters and communications on the business of the Society, and shall read to the Society all communications received by him as such Secretary. He shall, under the direction of the Society, prepare all communications to be addressed to others in the name of the Society, and keep true copies of the same.

8. The Librarian, under the direction of the Board of Managers, shall have the custody of the library and cabinet, including all manuscripts, papers, documents, coins and maps, and shall, under the

2

direction of the Board of Managers, provide cases suitable for their preservation, and for convenient reference and inspection. He shall keep a record of all donations, and report the same from time to time to the Society.

9. The Treasurer shall receive and keep all securities and sums of money due and payable or belonging to the Society. He shall keep the funds of the Society on deposit, to his credit as such Treasurer, in some safe institution, to be approved by the Board of Managers, and shall pay all such sums as the Board of Managers shall direct, on the written order or warrant of the President. He shall keep a true account of his receipts and disbursements, and render an annual statement thereof, and oftener if called upon by the Society or the Board of Managers. He may be required to give security for the faithful discharge of his duties, in such sum and form as the Board of Managers shall direct.

10. It shall be the duty of the Board of Managers to control and manage the affairs and funds of the Society. They shall make annually, on the second Tuesday of January, a report to the Society of its acquisitions and transactions for the preceding year.

11. All books, maps, manuscripts, and other articles belonging to the Society, shall be plainly marked with the name of the Society, and numbered, and entered in a catalogue arranged for convenient reference.

12. No books, maps, charts, manuscripts, or copies thereof, or any other article belonging to the library or cabinet, shall be taken therefrom without the written permission of a majority of the Board of Managers.

13. Any of these By-Laws may be suspended in case of a temporary exigency, by the unanimous vote of a meeting duly organized. They may be amended from time to time by a majority vote of the members present at a regular meeting, provided notice of the proposed amendment be given at least four weeks previous to a final vote thereon.

14. Any member of this Society may be expelled by the affirmative vote of two-thirds of all the resident members present at a regular meeting, but no such vote shall be taken unless notice of the motion to expel shall have been given at a meeting held at least four weeks previous thereto.

15. On the second Tuesday of January in each year, there shall be an address delivered before the Society, by some person to be appointed by the Board of Managers.

16. At the meetings of the Society, and (so far as may be applicable) at the meetings of the Board of Managers, the following shall be the order of business:

1. Reading of the minutes of the last meeting.
2. Reports and communications from the Officers of the Society.
3. Reports from Committees.
4. Election of members.
5. Miscellaneous business.
6. Reading of Papers and delivery of Addresses.

17. As soon as convenient after the annual election of officers, the President shall appoint from the Board of Managers, the following Standing Committees, to consist of three members each, viz.:

1. On Finance.
2. On the Library.
3. On Papers and Property.
4. On Donations, Subscriptions and Collections.
5. On Publications.
6. On Membership.

18. The President shall be, *ex officio*, Chairman of the Committee on Finance; and it shall be the duty of such Committee to take the general charge and supervision of the books, accounts, and reports of the Treasurer, and of the finances, receipts, and expenditures of the Society. It shall also be its duty to consider and recommend all suitable measures to increase the revenues of the Society, and promote economy in its expenditures. It shall examine and report upon all accounts and claims against the Society, and upon all propositions for the appropriation or expenditure of its funds, when such propositions have not been reported upon, or made, by some other Committee of the Board.

19. The Committee on the Library shall have the general charge and supervision of the Library, and of all propositions and measures in regard to its increase, use, and management; or in regard to the procurement, exchange, or other disposition of books, periodicals, and pamphlets, or their binding or preservation. They shall cause a full

and perfect catalogue of the books, periodicals, and pamphlets belonging to the same, to be made, and, from time to time, corrected, continued, and kept, in order to facilitate reference thereto, and secure proper accountability therefor.

20. The Committee on Papers and Property shall have the general charge and supervision of all the papers and other property of the Society which shall not be catalogued as a part of its Library, and thus placed in the special charge of the Committee on the Library Committee. It shall be its duty to cause a full and perfect list, or inventory of the same to be made, continued, and kept; and to propose to the Board, and carry into execution (after the approval of the Board of Managers has been obtained), such measures as may be deemed expedient for the classification, arrangement, care, preservation, and security of such papers, or, for obtaining papers or articles of historical or local interest for preservation by the Society.

21. The Committee on Donations, Subscriptions and Collections, shall have the general supervision and charge of procuring donations to the Society, and subscriptions to its funds, or for any special object. It shall also have charge of the collection thereof, and of all debts, and annual or other dues, to which the Society may be entitled; and it shall be its duty to propose proper measures for procuring donations and subscriptions, and for the prompt collection of all such subscriptions, debts and dues.

22. The Committee on Publications shall have the charge and supervision of all publications made by the direction of the Society, and shall carefully examine all papers and other things directed to be published, in order to discover all errors and defects, and procure the correction and remedy thereof. It shall also be their duty to make, or cause to be made, for publication, such abstracts or abridgments of papers as may be required, unless some other Committee shall have been charged with that duty.

23. It shall be the duty of the Committee on Membership to consider and report upon all questions relating to membership, which may be referred for that purpose, and, as far as practicable, to induce all proper persons to become members of the Society.

24. As soon as convenient after the annual election of officers, the President shall appoint the following Committees, each to consist of three members of the Society, not Managers, viz.:

1. On the Increase of the Library.
2. On the Increase of Members.
3. On Donations and Subscriptions.
4. On Statistics.
5. On Portraits, Pictures, and Photographs.
6. On Local History.
7. On Indian Reminiscences, Memorials, and History.

25. It shall be the duty of the Committee on the Increase of the Library, to procure donations of books and pamphlets; to endeavor, by other means, to increase the Library, and to propose to the Board of Managers such measures for its increase, as may be deemed expedient.

26. It shall be the duty of the Committee on the Increase of Members, to take all proper measures to increase the number of life and resident members; of the Committee on Donations and Subscriptions, to endeavor to increase the funds and property of the Society, by donations and legacies, and otherwise; of the Committee on Statistics, to collect, digest, arrange, and put in suitable form for preservation and use, the statistics of the commerce, manufactures, and business of the City of Buffalo and the Lakes, and of those portions of the West which are intimately connected with the business of Buffalo; of the Committee on Portraits, Pictures, and Photographs, to obtain donations of portraits, pictures and photographs, and especially of portraits, in oil, of early settlers and other citizens; of the Committee on Local History, to procure, digest, arrange, and put in proper order for preservation and use, materials for a history of the City of Buffalo, and of the several towns of the County of Erie; and of the Committee on Indian Reminiscences, Memorials and History, to discover, collect, and arrange in suitable form for preservation and use, whatever they can obtain relating to the habits, peculiarities, possessions, and history of the Indian Nations and Tribes, now, or formerly, occupying portions of this State.

27. All reports of Standing Committees shall be in writing, but they may report by resolution if they shall deem it expedient.

LIST OF OFFICERS OF THE SOCIETY

FROM ITS ORGANIZATION TO THE PRESENT TIME.

1862–1863.

MILLARD FILLMORE, ...	*President.*
LEWIS F. ALLEN, ...	*Vice-President.*
CHAS. D. NORTON, ...	*Recording Secretary.*
GUY H. SALISBURY, ...	*Cor. Sec'y and Librarian.*
OLIVER G. STEELE, ...	*Treasurer.*

1864.

MILLARD FILLMORE, ... *President.*
LEWIS F. ALLEN, ... *Vice-President.*
CHAS. D. NORTON, to March 8th, ...⎫
GEO. GORHAM, from March 8th, . . . ⎬ *Recording Secretary.*
GUY H. SALISBURY, to April 12th, . . .⎫
WM. K. SCOTT, from April 12th, ...⎬ *Cor. Sec'y and Librarian.*
OLIVER G. STEELE, ... *Treasurer.*

1865.

MILLARD FILLMORE, ... *President.*
LEWIS F. ALLEN, ... *Vice-President.*
GEO. GORHAM, to August 8th, ...⎫
S. S. ROGERS, from September 12th, . . .⎬ *Recording Secretary.*
WM. K. SCOTT, ... *Cor. Sec'y and Librarian.*
OLIVER G. STEELE, ... *Treasurer.*

1866.

MILLARD FILLMORE, ... *President.*
O. H. MARSHALL, ... *Vice-President.*
S. S. ROGERS, ... *Recording Secretary.*
WM. K. SCOTT, ... *Cor. Sec'y and Librarian.*
OLIVER G. STEELE, ... *Treasurer.*

1867.

MILLARD FILLMORE,	*President.*
O. H. MARSHALL,	*Vice-President.*
WM. C. BRYANT,	*Recording Secretary.*
GEORGE S. ARMSTRONG,	*Cor. Sec'y and Librarian.*
OLIVER G. STEELE,	*Treasurer.*

1868.

HENRY W. ROGERS,	*President.*
ALBERT T. CHESTER, D. D.	*Vice-President.*
WM. C. BRYANT,	*Recording Secretary.*
GEORGE S. ARMSTRONG,	*Cor. Sec'y and Librarian.*
OLIVER G. STEELE,	*Treasurer.*

1869.

ALBERT T. CHESTER, D. D.,	*President.*
ORSAMUS H. MARSHALL,	*Vice-President.*
WM. C. BRYANT,	*Recording Secretary.*
GEO. S. ARMSTRONG,	*Cor. Sec'y and Librarian.*
OLIVER G. STEELE,	*Treasurer.*

1870.

ORSAMUS H. MARSHALL,	*President.*
GEO. R. BABCOCK,	*Vice-President.*
WM. C. BRYANT,	*Recording Secretary.*
GEO. S. ARMSTRONG,	*Cor. Sec'y and Librarian.*
WARREN BRYANT,	*Treasurer.*

1871.

NATHAN K. HALL,	*President.*
WM. H. GREENE,	*Vice-President.*
WM. C. BRYANT,	*Recording Secretary.*
GEO. S. ARMSTRONG,	*Cor. Sec'y and Librarian.*
OLIVER G. STEELE,	*Treasurer.*

1872.

WM. H. GREENE,	*President.*
ORLANDO ALLEN,	*Vice-President.*
WM. C. BRYANT,	*Recording Secretary.*
GEO. S. ARMSTRONG,	*Cor. Sec'y and Librarian.*
GEO. S. ARMSTRONG,	*Treasurer.*

16

1873.

ORLANDO ALLEN, ... *President.*
OLIVER G. STEELE, ... *Vice-President.*
WM. C. BRYANT, ... *Recording Secretary.*
GEO. S. ARMSTRONG, ... *Cor. Sec'y and Librarian.*
GEO. S. ARMSTRONG, ... *Treasurer.*

1874.

OLIVER G. STEELE, ... *President.*
JAMES SHELDON, ... *Vice-President.*
WM. C. BRYANT, ... *Recording Secretary.*
GEO. S. ARMSTRONG, ... *Cor. Sec'y and Librarian.*
GEO. S. ARMSTRONG, ... *Treasurer.*

OFFICERS OF THE SOCIETY

FOR 1875.

JAMES SHELDON, ... *President.*
WM. C. BRYANT, ... *Vice-President.*
ELIAS O. SALISBURY, ... *Recording Secretary.*
GEO. S. ARMSTRONG, ... *Cor. Sec'y and Librarian.*
GEO. S. ARMSTRONG, ... *Treasurer.*

COUNCILLORS.

PASCAL P. PRATT,	ORSAMUS H. MARSHALL,	WM. P. LETCHWORTH,
REV. A. T. CHESTER, D.D.	HENRY MARTIN,	WM. H. H. NEWMAN,
WM. H. GREENE,	FRANCIS H. ROOT,	OLIVER G. STEELE.

STANDING COMMITTEES OF THE BOARD OF MANAGERS.

Finance.—The President, *ex officio*, Chairman ; Henry Martin, Pascal P. Pratt, Oliver G. Steele.

Library.—Rev. Albert T. Chester, Orsamus H. Marshall, William H. Greene.

Papers and Property.—William C. Bryant, William P. Letchworth, Elias O. Salisbury.

Donations and Collections.—Oliver G. Steele, Francis H. Root, Pascal P. Pratt.

Publications.—William H. H. Newman, Orsamus H. Marshall, Albert T. Chester.

Membership.—William H. Greene, George S. Armstrong, Henry Martin.

STANDING COMMITTEES OF THE SOCIETY.

On the Increase of the Library.—Alonzo Richmond, William H. Glenny, James McCredie.

On Increase of Members.—Eurotus Marvin, John Sage, George P. Stevenson.

On Donations and Subscriptions.—Warren Bryant, Gibson T. Williams, William K. Allen.

On Portraits, Pictures and Photographs.—Geo. S. Hazard, E. C. Sprague, S. S. Rogers.

On Statistics.—Henry Childs, E. P. Dorr, John R. Lee.

On Local History.—Julius E. Francis, Charles E. Young, Myron P. Bush.

On Indian Reminiscences, etc.—John S. Ganson, Rev. Albert Bigelow, Lorenzo D. Gould.

3

COLLECTIONS OF THE SOCIETY.

Autograph Letters from Paul Busti and others, to Joseph Ellicott, agent of the Holland Land Company, relating to the business of the said company, from May 18, 1799 to March 15, 1822. The letters for 1807-8 and 9, are missing. In two bound volumes, pp. 650 and 1164. Presented by Professor Ellicott Evans, of Hamilton College.

Autograph Letters, Memoranda and Statements, written and sent to Joseph Ellicott, relating to the business of the Holland Land Company, from July 22, 1795 to December 3, 1810. In two bound volumes, pp. 826 and 1248. Presented by Professor Ellicott Evans.

Autograph Letters written to Joseph Ellicott by the settlers on the Holland Land Purchase and others, relating to the business of the Holland Land Company, from January 3, 1802 to December 9, 1819. In sixteen volumes.

Autograph Political and Miscellaneous Letters, written by various parties to Joseph Ellicott, from December 13, 1814 to September 15, 1821. In one bound volume, pp. 812. Presented by Professor Ellicott Evans.

Copies of Letters written by Joseph Ellicott to various parties, relating to the business of the Holland Land Company, from November 26, 1800 to August 3, 1821. In three bound volumes, pp. 370, 870, and 520. Presented by Professor Ellicott Evans.

Original Land Ledger kept by the Holland Land Company, comprising the accounts with the various purchasers of the Inner and Outer lots in the village of New Amsterdam, now City of Buffalo, commencing August 1, 1804. In one bound volume, pp. 488.

Original Contracts or "Articles" between the Holland Land Company and the settlers, from October 1, 1799 to September 11, 1806, embracing the said Inner and Outer lots. In two bound volumes containing 209 contracts. Also the duplicates of the above "articles" which were surrendered by the settlers on receiving their deeds.

Manuscript Journal and Memoranda of Transactions relating to the business of the Holland Land Company, from January 2, 1801 to January 1, 1813. In two bound volumes, pp. 254 and 250. Presented by David E. E. Mix.

Autograph Journal kept by the Hon. Henry R. Storrs, while Member of Congress from Oneida County, containing an account of political occurrences from December 22, 1825 to May 16, 1830. In six manuscript bound volumes. Presented by William C. Storrs, Esq.

Manuscript Account, by the Rev. Jabez B. Hyde, first missionary to the Senecas, of the Seneca Mission and the progress of Christianity among the Senecas. Dated August 28, 1820. In one bound folio volume of 31 pages. Presented by the Hon. Joseph W. Moulton.

Autograph Journal, kept by Major James Norris, of the expedition of Gen. Sullivan against the Senecas in 1779. One bound volume, pp. 94. Presented by the Hon. Joseph Williamson, of Belfast, Maine.

Manuscript Autograph Narrative, by the Hon. Augustus Porter, of events connected with the early settlement of Western New York, with a manuscript map of the Phelps and Gorham Purchase. Dated March 11, 1848. In one bound volume of 110 pages.

Copy of the Parish Register of St. Mark's Church in Niagara, Canada, containing a Record of Births and Marriages in said Parish, from 1792 to 1829, accompanied by an interesting descriptive article contributed by Wm. C. Bryant, Esq. Presented by Geo. B. Ketchum.

Autograph Manuscripts of Dr. Francis Adrian Vanderkemp, comprising his notices of Buffon's and Jefferson's theories in Natural History. His Autobiography written in 1817. Memoir on the Use of Copper by the Greeks. Tour from the Hudson to Lake Ontario, by the way of the Mohawk River, Oneida Lake and Oswego River in 1792. Also numerous Autograph Letters of Presidents Adams and Jefferson, Governors George and De Witt Clinton, Aaron Burr, and other persons of distinction. Presented by Mrs. Pauline E. Henry, of Philadelphia, granddaughter of Dr. Vanderkemp.

Printed and Manuscript Maps. Those on rollers are arranged on a frame, and those in sheets numbered and placed in proper order, in large books, and indexed, so that they can all be examined with great facility.

Obituary Record This commences in 1811, and embraces the names, ages, and dates of death, alphabetically arranged, of all citizens of the age of twenty years and upwards, being over 12,000, whose deaths have been published in the Buffalo papers.

Marriage Record. This embraces all the marriages which have been announced in the Buffalo papers since the year 1811, including the names of the parties in alphabetical order, the dates of marriage in chronological order, and the names of the journals in which they were published. Every entry is necessarily repeated, so as to be alphabetically arranged under the surname of each party.

These two records of deaths and marriages will at all times be accessible to the public, without charge, and will often save hours of perhaps fruitless search among voluminous files of papers.

The Collection of Pamphlets, embracing over 4,500, carefully arranged in one hundred and thirty-seven cases, and indexed, is quite valuable, for a large portion of which the Society is indebted to its first president, the Hon. Millard Fillmore, it being the accumulation of his entire political life.

Bound Books. The collection is yet small, embracing about 4,800 volumes. Among them are many rare Historical Works.

Autograph Signatures and Letters. The collection is valuable, embracing many letters of distinguished characters, all carefully arranged and indexed.

48 Oil Portraits of citizens, and others of life-size, and

142 Photographs of cabinet size, all arranged on the walls of the Library.

290 Photographs of smaller size arranged in albums and alphabetically indexed.

The Society is the depository of many valuable Manuscripts besides those enumerated, Indian Relics, Trophies and Mementoes of the recent war, and other articles too numerous for detailed description.

BUFFALO DAILY NEWSPAPERS IN BOUND VOLUMES.

Buffalo Commercial Advertiser, from 1835 to 1875.

Buffalo Daily Courier, from 1842 to 1875.

Buffalo Morning Express, from 1848 to 1868, 1873 to 1875.

Buffalo Daily Republic, from 1847 to 1854, 1858 to 1859.

The Daily Democracy, from November 11, 1854 to May 9, 1855.

Buffalo Daily Journal, from March 21, 1836 to February 22, 1837.

Buffalo Daily Gazette, from March 2, 1843 to February 11, 1845.

Daily National Pilot, from February 12, 1845 to June 30, 1846.

The Morning Advertiser, from April 7, 1855 to November 17, 1855.

Buffalo Courier and Economist, from 1842 to 1844.

Evening Courier and Republic, from January 2 to June 30, 1862 ; January 2 to December 31, 1863.

BUFFALO WEEKLY NEWSPAPERS IN BOUND VOLUMES.

Buffalo Weekly Express, 1854, 1856 to 1858, 1859 to 1862.

Buffalo Weekly Republic, from 1848 to 1850, 1857, 1858 ; January 4 to August 30, 1859.

Buffalo Weekly Journal, from July 24, 1827 to November 10, 1829; December 29, 1829 to March 30, 1831.

B ffalo Weekly Journal and General Advertiser, from December 29, 1829 to March 30, 1831.

Buffalo Whig and Journal, from June 18, 1834 to January 6, 1836.

Buffalo Patriot and Commercial Advertiser, from January 14, 1834 to November 22, 1837.

Buffalo Emporium, from September 24, 1824 to March 21, 1829.

Black Rock Advocate, from February 11, 1836 to February 3, 1837.

Black Rock Beacon, from January 9, 1822 to April 8, 1824.

Literary Inquirer, vols. 1 and 2, from January 1, 1833 to October 15, 1834.

BUFFALO MONTHLY BOUND VOLUME.

" For Everybody," vol. 1, from February to December, 1871.

CLUB MEETINGS.

———◦•————

Soon after the organization of the Society, a system of Club meetings was instituted, which have continued to be held during the winter months at private residences by invitation of members. It has been customary at each meeting to have an appropriate Paper read, followed by such remarks and discussion as the subject might suggest. These meetings, in their informal and social character, have proved a valuable addition to the constitutional machinery of the Society, and have exercised a marked influence in promoting historical research among the members.

The following is a list of the Papers, with the names of the authors and the dates when read. Their number and character fully justify the wisdom and expediency of this auxiliary organization.

Those marked thus † have not been deposited with the Society.

DATE.		AUTHOR.	SUBJECT.
1863.			
Jan.	23	O. G. Steele,	Buffalo Common Schools.
Feb.	3	O. H. Marshall,	The site where La Salle built the " Griffin."
	3	Guy H. Salisbury,	Buffalo in 1836 and 1862.
	3	Alden S. Stevens,	First Town Meeting on the H. Purchase in 1803.
	13	Geo. R. Babcock,	Origin of the name of Black Rock.
Mch.	3	Wm. A. Bird,	Charters and boundaries of N. Y. and adj'g States.
	3	Curtis L. Brace,	" Golden Wedding " of Mr. and Mrs. Lester Brace.
	3	John A. Vinton,	†Mission among the Indians in Western New York.
	13	Wm. Dorsheimer,	†On the War of 1812.
	13	David Gray,	Poem : Extermination of the Kah Kwahs.
Apl.	7	Wm. Ketchum,	Origin of the name of Black Rock.
	7	Wm. A. Bird,	Origin of the name of Buffalo City.
June	2	Henry Wells,	History of the American Express Company.
July	14	N. T. Strong,	Traditionary Origin of the name of Buffalo.
Aug.	14	Wm. Ketchum,	†Letter controverting the above.
Sept.	8	Edw'd Huntington,	†Record of Canal tolls at Rome, 1813-20.
	8	N. T. Strong,	Letter as to Origin of the name of Buffalo.
Nov.	17	Lewis F. Allen,	Rise and Fall of the Great Lakes.
	23	C. F. S. Thomas,	The Buffalo Press from 1835 to 1863.
	30	Guy H. Salisbury,	Early history of the Press of Erie County.
Dec.	14	Charles D. Norton,	The Old Ferry at Black Rock.
	21	Geo. V. Brown,	Voyage of a vessel from L. Erie to Morocco.
	28	E. S. Prosser,	Enlargement of Locks of the Erie Canal.

DATE.	AUTHOR.	SUBJECT.
1864.		
Jan. 4	E. P. Dorr,	History of our Lake Commerce.
13	Geo. W. Hosmer,	Physiognomy of Buffalo.
21	L. G. Sellstedt,	Life and Character of Wm. J. Wilgus.
25	Jno. Wilkeson,	Manufacture of Iron in Buffalo.
Feb. 1	Wm. A. Bird,	Boundary survey between the U. States and Canada.
15	O. G. Steele,	Biographical sketch of Walter Joy.
15	Chas. D. Norton,	Biographical sketch of Silas Sawin.
22	O. Stiles,	†Memoir of Judge James Mullett.
29	Guy H. Salisbury,	Our Lake Marine: by Capt. A. Walker.
Mch. 14	E. P. Dorr,	Insurance.
21	A. Bradish,	†Memoir of Dr. Douglas Houghton.
28	A. R. Ketchum.	Account of the Buffalo Water-Works.
28	Geo. W. Clinton,	Obituary notice of Edward S. Warren.
28	Jno. B. Skinner,	Obituary notice of Judge James G. Hoyt.
May 10	Henry Lovejoy,	On the Early History of Buffalo.
Dec. 10	Henry Daw,	The building of the "Walk-in-the-Water."
26	Ellicott Evans,	Reminiscences of Joseph Ellicott.
1865.		
Jan. 6	Wm. Dorsheimer,	Biographical sketch of Thomas C. Welch.
, 6	N. K. Hall,	The Postal Service connected with Buffalo.
16	Richard Williams,	Black Rock Harbor, Pier, Water-power, and F. Mills.
21	Elijah D. Efner,	His Autobiog'phy; War of 1812; Sketches of Buffalo.
23	Chas. D. Norton,	History of Old Fort Schlosser, etc.
Feb. 6	H. W. Rogers,	Biographical notice of Henry Daw.
6	L. F. Allen,	His residence in the West from 1818 to 1821.
13	Thomas Blossom,	Office of the Holland Land Co. in Buffalo.
13	Mary W. Palmer,	Narrative of the loss of the "Walk-in-the-Water."
13	Millard Fillmore,	Biographical sketch of Asa Rice.
20	Geo. W. Holley,	†Sortie of Fort Erie.
20	Millard Fillmore,	Biographical sketch of Joseph Clary.
27	O. H. Marshall,	Early His. and Local Names of Niagara Frontier.
27	Wm. A. Bird,	Letter on the "Sortie of Fort Erie."
Mch. 6	W. G. Morton,	†Discovery of anæsthetical properties of Ether.
13	Joseph Dart,	History of Elevators.
20	C. F. S. Thomas,	History of Music in Buffalo.
27	Fred. S. Cozzens,	Memoir of Col. Peter A. Porter.
27	Albert H. Porter,	Niagara Falls and vicinity since 1800.
Apl. 3	Horace V. Soper,	†History of the Ketchum Mowing Machine.
3	Miss Ann Powell,	Journal fr. Ft. Niagara to Ft. Erie and Buff. Cr. in 1789.
July 11	Wm. Ketchum,	Memorial of George Coit.
Apl. 3	Orange Dean,	†The Indians of the Six Nations.
June 20	Geo. R. Babcock,	Memorial of George Palmer.
Oct. 10	L. F. Allen,	†Early forwarding merchants of B. Rock and Buffalo.
Dec. 4	Geo. W. Hosmer,	History of a New England town.
18	L. F. Allen,	†Cholera in Buffalo in 1832.
1866.		
Jan. 3	O. G. Steele,	City Sewerage and Sanitary Science.
15	Wm. C. Young,	Reminiscences of the Erie Canal Survey in 1817.
29	Wm. A. Bird,	Early transportation from Albany to Buffalo.
Feb. 6	N. K. Hall,	Biographical sketch of S. G. Haven.
21	M. S. Hawley,	Origin of the Erie Canal.
Mch. 8	L. F. Allen,	Ararat on Grand Island, and the "Corner Stone."
8	Wm. H. Greene,	Biographical sketch of Thomas T. Sherwood.
20	James L. Barton,	Early Reminiscences of Buffalo and vicinity.
27	J. R. Lothrop,	Ozone.

Date.	Author.	Subject.
1866.		
Mch. 27	Geo. W. Hosmer,	Biographical sketch of Rev. Wm. Stiell Brown.
May 8	Joseph Ellicott,	Letter of, to Simeon De Witt, on Inland Navigation.
8	Wm. Dorsheimer,	†Biographical sketch of Albert H. Tracy.
1867.		
Jan. 7	Richard Williams,	Observations in the Great Valley of the West.
21	Lewis A. Morgan,	†Indian Architecture.
24	John C. Lord,	Annual Historical Address.
28	George Geddes,	Origin of the Erie Canal.
Feb. 18	Thos. C. Pitkin,	†French and English contest for the State of N. York.
Mch. 4	G. H. Goodrich,	The Old Houses of Buffalo.
4	Theodotus Burwell,	†Buffalo Lyceum and N. Y. State Normal School Syst.
4	Elliott W. Stewart,	Old wreck and stockade near Eighteen Mile Creek.
4	O. H. Marshall,	Wreck of the "Beaver" in 1763, near Eighteen M. C.
Apl. 1	L. L. Doty,	Sullivan's Expedition against the Senecas.
16	H. K. Viele,	On the Life of H. K. Smith.
1868.		
Jan. 30	O. G. Steele,	Presentation of the portrait of Red Jacket.
Feb. 3	M. S. Hawley,	The Erie Canal; Its Origin, Success and Necessity.
18	Jas. O. Putnam,	On the Life of Harvey Putnam.
Mch. 2	Orlando Allen,	†Sketches of Red Jacket and other Indians.
16	Samuel Sizer,	†Last days and notices of Baron Steuben.
1869.		
Jan. 11	Theodotus Burwell,	Reminiscences of the Bar of Erie Co.
25	John S. Trowbridge,	Memoir of Dr. Josiah Trowbridge.
Feb. 15	G. Naphegyi,	Languages of the American Aborigines.
Mch. 1	James Sheldon,	Reminiscences, General and Local, 1817–18.
1	Nathaniel Wilgus,	Military Expedition to Grand Island in 1819.
15	George E. Hayes,	Geology of Buffalo.
15	Nathaniel Wilgus,	On the Execution of the Three Thayers.
29	H. G. White,	Reminiscences of Buffalo since 1836.
Apl. 5	A. T. Chester,	On the Life of Col. Benjamin Hodge.
13	Orlando Allen,	†On the Six Nations of New York.
1870.		
Jan. 31	Peter Barker,	Early History of the Town of Evans.
Feb. 25	Henry W. Rogers,	†Wits of the Buffalo Bar. First Paper.
Mch. 4	Henry W. Rogers,	†Wits of the Buffalo Bar. Second Paper.
7	Wm. H. C. Hosmer,	Annals of "Hartford," now Avon, Livingston Co.
Dec. 5	Geo. W. Clinton,	On the late Commodore Stephen Champlin.
19	L. G. Sellstedt,	On the late Roswell W. Haskins.
1871.		
Jan. 5	Orlando Allen,	†Personal Reminiscences of the Author.
16	Wm. A. Bird,	†On the History of Steam.
31	Wm. H. Greene,	Sketch of Judge Horatio J. Stow.
Feb. 14	S. S. Rogers,	On the late Charles D. Norton.
21	G. W. Holley,	Niagara; Its Geology, History, Incidents and Poetry.
Mch. 7	David Gray,	On the late Guy H. Salisbury.
Apl. 11	David E. E. Mix,	Incidents relating to the Holland Purchase.
1872.		
Jan. 4	O. G. Steele,	Incidents of Travel in Russia.
Feb. 12	J. C. Lord,	On the late Samuel Wilkeson.
26	V. R. Hotchkiss,	†Voyage down the Volga.
Mch. 11	V. R. Hotchkiss,	†Voyage from Tzaritzin to Constantinople.
25	A. T. Chester,	On the late Dr. Walter Clarke.
1873.		
Jan. 13	V. R. Hotchkiss,	†Observations and Experiences in Constantinople.
27	David Gray,	†Historical Sketch of Robert Burns.

Date.	Author.	Subject.
1873.		
Feb. 10	Mrs. Kate Osborn,	†Sketches of the Life of Joseph Brant.
24	Jas. O. Putnam,	Life of Hon. John B. Skinner.
Mch. 10	Wm. P. Letchworth,	On the late Samuel F. Pratt.
24	A. T. Chester,	†A Trip to Nova Scotia.
Dec. 16	A. T. Chester,	†The " Boston Tea Party."
1874.		
Jan. 5	E. P. Dorr,	Origin and History of the " Monitor."
19	T. M. Bishop.	†Early History of Seneca County.
Feb. 2	C. O. Shepard,	†Cultivation of the Tea Plant.
16	A. Bigelow,	†The old firm of Juba Storrs & Co.
Mch. 16	O. H. Marshall,	La Salle's visit to the Senecas in 1669.
30	Jas. O. Putnam,	On the late Judge N. K. Hall.
Apl. 13	L. J. Fletcher,	The True Site of the Holy Sepulchre.
Jan. 11	A. T. Chester,	The Battle of New Orleans.
1875.		
25	James Sheldon,	Biographical sketch of Oliver Forward.
Feb. 8	L. Van Bokkelen,	†Pioneer History of the Genesee Valley.
22	Wm. Hodge,	†Life and Times of Wm. Hodge, senior.
Mch. 8	James W. Ward,	†Library of the British Museum.
22	L. W. Miller,	†Personal Reminiscences of the Canadian Rebellion.
Apl. 5	Geo. W. Clinton,	†On his Father, De Witt Clinton.

ANNUAL MEMBERS

Abell, William H.
Adams, S. Cary,
Alberger, William C.
Albro, James,
Allen, John, Jr.
Allen, William K.
*Anderson, Alexander S.
†Arey, Rev. Charles,
Armstrong, George S.
Auchinvole, John,
*Austin, Benjamin H.
*Baker, Albert L.
Baker, Howard H.
Bancroft, Samuel B.
Barnes, Dr. Edwin R.
Barnum, George G.
Barnum, Stephen O.
Beals, George,
Beard, Daniel C.
Bell, David,
Bemis, Asaph S.
Bennett, Edward,
†Benton, Rev. A. L.
Best, Robert H.
Beyer, Philip,
Bigelow, Rev. Albert,
Bills, Rev. J. E.
Birge, Martin H.
Bishop, Rev. E. R.
Bishop, Rev. T. M.
Blanchard, Amos A.
Blossom, Thomas,
*Bogert, Lawrence K.
*Bogue, Rev. H. P.
Bork, Joseph,
Bowen, Daniel,
*Brace, Curtis L.
†Brennan, Barnabas H.
Brown, R. N.
Brunck, Dr. Francis C.
Bryan, George J.
Bryant, George H.
Bryant, Warren,
*Buchanan, R. G.
Buckham, Rev. H. B.
*Bull, Absalom,
Bull, George W.
Bull, William S.
Bullymore, Richard,
Burrows, Roswell L.
Burtis, Peter P.

Burwell, Dr. George N.
Calkins, Rev. Wolcott,
Carmichael, Robert,
*Caryl, Benjamin C.
*Chamberlin, Samuel M.
Champlin, O. H. P.
Chapin, Cooley S.
Chapin, John R.
Cheesman, William,
Chester, Rev. A. T., D. D.
Chester, Leonard H.
Chester, Thomas,
Childs, Henry,
Chivers, Rev. E. E.
Church, Alvah,
Clapp, A. M.
Clark, Cyrus,
Clark, Delavan F.
*Clark, John W.
Clarke, Charles S.
*Clarke, Rev. Walter, D. D.
Clinton, George W.
Coatsworth, Thomas,
Cobb, Lorenzo D.
*Cochrane, A. G. C.
Cook, Josiah,
Cook, Rev. P. G.
*Cornwell, Francis E.
Cothran, George W.
Cowing, John H.
Coye, Schuyler,
Crumb, Dr. William R.
Cunningham, Henry S.
Curtis, Fred B.
*Cutter, Ammi W.
Daboll, G. C.
Danforth, Frederick L.
Dann, Edward S.
Darrow, Charles B.
Darrow, Noyes,
Dart, Erastus D.
Dart, Joseph,
*Daw, Henry,
Day, David F.
Day, Hiram C.
Dean, Bradford C.
De Forest, Cyrus H.
Dick, Rev. Alexander,
Dick, Rev. Robert,
Dodge, Hampton,
*Dorsheimer, Philip,

Drullard, Solomon,
Dudley, Joseph D.
Dudley, Joseph P.
Dunbar, Robert,
*Efner, Elijah D.
Elder, Stewart,
Emslie, Peter,
Enos, George T.
*Enos, Laurens,
Eustaphieve, Alexander A.
Evans, Charles W.
Evans, Edwin T.
Evans, James C.
Evans, Lewis M.
Fairchild, Joseph L.
Falk, Rev. S.
Farnham, Ammi,
Farnham, Thomas,
Farrar, Chilian M.
Farwell, H. D.
Felton, John,
Ferris, Peter J.
Fields, Samuel H.
Fisher, George,
Fisher, J. H.
*Fiske, William,
*Flagg, Samuel D.
Fleming, William,
Fletcher, Rev. J. L.
Fobes, William Dana,
Folwell, Dr. Mahlon B.
*Forbush, Eliakim B.
Ford, James E.
Fowler, James S.
Fox, Watson A.
Francis, Daniel,
Fraser, Rev. David R.
French, Thomas B.
Fullerton, James C.
*Gallagher, Frank B.
*Galligan, William,
*Ganson, John S.
*Gardner, Noah H.
Garrett, Cuyler,
Gay, Rev. William A.
Germain, Charles B.
Gilbert, Edwin,
Glenny, William H.
Gould, Lorenzo D.
Graves, John C.
Gray, David,

* Deceased.   † Removed.

4

Greene, William H.
Grey, Ernst G.
*Grosvenor, Seth H.
Gurney, William H.
Haight, Albert,
Hale, Rev. C. S.
Hall, Edward J.
Hall, Nathaniel,
Hamlen, Robert D.
Hamlin, Charles W.
*Harvey, Alexander W.
Harvey, Dr. Leon F.
Hathaway, Isaac T.
Hawks, Thomas S.
Hawley, Elias S.
Hayes, George B.
Hayes, George E.
Hazard, Edward E.
Hazard, George S.
*Hazard, Morris,
Heacock, Rev. G.W., D. D.
Hearne, Henry,
Hedge, Charles L.
Hedstrom, E. L.
Hefford, R. R.
Henderson, Rev. John M.
Hersee, Thompson,
Heywood, Russell H.
Hill, Dr. John D.
*Hodge, Benjamin,
Hodge, William,
Holland, Nelson,
Holloway, Isaac,
Holmes, Britton,
Hopkins, Dr. Henry R.
Horton, John M.
Hotchkiss, Rev.V. R., D.D.
Howard, Austin A.
Howard, Rufus L.
Howell, John,
Howland, Henry R.
*Hoyt, James G.
Hubbard, Linus,
Hume, Stevenson.
Hunt, Rev. S.
†Hutchins, Rev. Charles L.
Hutchinson, John M.
†Ingersoll, Rev. Edw. D. D.
Inglehart, Frederick,
Ives, William,
Jewett, Josiah,
*Jones, George,
*Joy, Walter,
Keating, Robert,
Keller, Henry D.
Kendall, Rev. C.
Kent, Henry M.
Kenyon, Dr. L. M.
*Ketchum, Jesse,

King, William, Jr.
Kingsley, Silas,
Kip, Henry,
Kniest, Rev. John B.
Lacy, John T.
Lansing, Henry L.
Larned, J. N.
Laverack, William,
Lawrence, S. N.
Lee, Cyrus P.
*Lee, George F.
Lee, James H.
Lee, R. Porter,
Lewis, L. L.
Locke, Franklin D.
Longstreet, Christopher,
*Loomis, Charles K.
Loomis, Charles T.
Loomis, Dr. Horatio N.
Loomis, Thomas,
Lord, Rev. J. C., D. D.
*Lothrop, Dr. J. R.
*Lovejoy, Henry,
Lyman, William E.
Lynde, B. A.
Lyon, James S.
Lyon, William W.
Madison, James H.
†Marshall, Rev. B. D.
Marshall, Charles D.
Martin, Frank,
Martin, V. R.
Marvin, George L.
Matteson, Harry H.
Matteson, P. A.
Mayhew, Jonathan,
Maynard, Robert H.
McCredie, James,
†McLean, Rev. Alexander.
*Meech, Asa B.
Miller, Capt. Frederick S.
Miner, Dr. Julius F.
*Monteath, William,
Montgomery, Henry,
Montgomery, Hugh,
Montgomery, Robert,
Moore, John H.
Moore, Mark B.
Morey, Norris,
Morgan, Darwin E.
†Muller, Rev. D. H.
Norton, Charles D.
Noye, John T.
Noye, Richard K.
Noyes, John S.
Ottenot, Nicholas,
Otto, John,
Ovens, Robert,
. Ovens, Walter S.

*Palmer, George,
Park, Paul,
Parke, James B.
Pattison, Francis G.
Pease, Frank S.
Pease, John,
Peck, William B.
*Perkins, Thomas G.
Pierce, Jerome,
*Plimpton, Luman K.
*Porter, Peter A.
Pratt, Frederick L.
*Pratt, Dr. Gorham F.
Putnam, James O.
Randall, Adley,
Randall, Milton,
Reed, Rev. William,
Remington, Cyrus K.
Rice, William S.
*Rich, Andrew J.
Rich, G. Barrett,
Richmond, Alonzo,
Richmond, Henry A.
Richmond, Jewett M.
Riester, Fernando J.
Ripley, Rev. A. P.
Robertson, George W.
*Robie, Rev. John E.
*Robinson, Coleman T.
Robson, J. O.
Rogers, B. D.
Rogers, Sherman S.
Rogers, Gen. William F.
*Rounds, George W.
Rumrill, Henry,
Sage, John,
Salisbury, Elias O.
Saunders, P. D. K.
*Sawin, Silas,
Scatcherd, James N.
Schermerhorn, Rev. M. K.
Schryver, Allen L.
Scott, George W.
Scoville, John,
Scoville, N. C.
Scroggs, Gustavus A.
*Sexton, Jason,
*Seymour, Horatio,
Sheldon, James,
Shelton, Rev. Wm., D. D.
Sheppard, James D.
Sherman, Robert D.
*Sherwood, Albert,
Sherwood, William C.
Shoecraft, James P.
*Shumway, Horatio,
Sicard, George J.
Sidway, Franklin,
Sigison, George W.

Sill, Edward E.
Simson, Andrew,
Smith, Moses,
Smith, Patrick,
Smith, Samuel,
*Snow, R. G.
Southwick, Alfred P.
Sprague, E. C.
Stearns, George C.
Stebbins, William H.
*Sternburgh, Pearl L.
Stillman, Horace,
Stowitz, George H.
Stringer, George A.
Strong, John C.
Strong, P. H., M. D.
Strobridge, Rev. Geo. E.
†Stuart, Rev. D. M.
Sweet, Charles A.
Sweet, Lorenzo,
Taber, William D.
Tanner, Alonzo,
Taylor, Augustus C.
Taylor, Martin,
Thompson, A. P.
Thornton, Thomas,
Tifft, John V.

Tilden, J. H.
Toles, Benjamin,
Tripp, A. F.
Tuthill, E. D.
Tweedy, William,
Tyler, John,
Urban, George,
*Utley, Horace,
Vail, George O.
Van Bokkelen, Rev. L.D.D.
Van Buren, James,
Van Dyke, Rev. L. B.
*Verplanck, Isaac A.
Vosburg, William H.
Vought, John H.
Wadsworth, George,
Walbridge, Charles E.
Walker, Henry C.
Walls, John,
Ward, Rev. Henry,
Ward, James W.
Wardwell, George S.
*Warren, Edward S.
Warren, Joseph,
Watson, S. V. R.
*Weatherby, John L.
Webster, Ellis,

Welch, Samuel M.
*Wells, Richard H.
Weppner, Arnold,
*Wheeler, Rufus,
White, Rev. A. D.
†White, E. N.
*White, Henry A.
*White, Isaac D.
White, John,
*Wilgus, Nathaniel,
Wilkeson, John,
Willett, James M.
Williams, Benjamin H.
Williams, Frank,
Williams, Richard,
Williams, William,
Williams, William J.
Wilson, Guilford R.
Wilson, Leonard,
Wilson, Robert P.
Wolfsohn, R. W.
Wood, Rev. Charles,
Wood, Francis P.
Woodrow, Rev. S. G.
Wright, Alfred P.
Wyckoff, Dr. C. C.

LIFE MEMBERS.

Allen, Lewis F.
*Allen, Orlando,
*Austin, Stephen G.
Babcock, George R.
Beals, Edward P.
Becker, Philip,
Bird, William A.
Bowen, Dennis,
Box, Henry W.
Brayley, James,
Bryant, William C.
*Burwell, Mrs. Maria T.
Bush, Myron P.
Cary, Walter,
Chandler, Henry,
Clark, Thomas,
Clement, Stephen M.

Coit, George, Jr.
Colie, Samuel D.
Cornell, Samuel G.
Dakin, George,
Deshler, John G.
Dobbins, David P.
Dorr, E. P.
Dorsheimer, William
Ensign, Charles,
Fargo, William G.
*Fillmore, Millard,
Fillmore, M. Powers,
Francis, Julius E.
†Frothingham, Rev. Fred.
*Ganson, John,
Guthrie, S. S.
*Hall, Nathan K.

Hamlin, Cicero J.
Hawley, Merwin S.
Hibbard, George B.
Howard, Ethan H.
Howard, George,
Hudson, John T.
Jewett, Elam R.
Jewett, Sherman S.
Lacy, John T., Jr.
Lee, John R.
Letchworth, William P.
Lovering, William, Jr.
Marsh, Phineas S.
Marshall, Orsamus H.
Martin, Henry,
Marvin, Eurotus,
Miller, William F.

* Deceased. † Removed.

Morgan, Amos,
Morse, David R.
Newman, William H. H.
Nichols, Asher P.
Parker, Perry G.
Pratt, Pascal P.
*Pratt, Samuel F.
Prosser, Erastus S.
Ramsdell, Orrin P.
Rochester, Thomas F.
Rockwell, Augustus,
Rogers, Henry W.
Root, Francis H.
*Rumsey, Aaron,

Rumsey, Bronson C.
Rumsey, Dexter P.
*Salisbury, Guy H.
Sawyer, James D.
Scott, William K.
Sellstedt, L. G.
Shepard, John D.
Sherman, Richard J.
*Skinner, John B.
Smith, James M.
Spaulding, E. G.
Steele, Oliver G.
Stevenson, Edward L.
Stevenson, George P.

Sweeney, James,
†Thomas, C. F. S.
Tifft, George W.
Tracy, Francis W.
Walker, Wm. H.
*Welch, Thomas C.
Wells, Chandler H.
White, Charles H.
White, George W.
White, Henry G.
White, James P.
Williams, Gibson T.
Woodruff, L. C.
Young, Charles E.

--- • --- • ---------

CORRESPONDING MEMBERS.

--- • ---

Aigin, James, Delaware, Ohio.
*Allen, Richard L., New York.
Alvord, Hon. Thos. G., Syracuse.
Andrews, Prof. E. B., Marietta, Ohio.
Atwood, Henry, Lancaster.
*Babcock, James F., New Haven, Ct.
Babcock, Marcus L., Batavia.
Bacon, Leonard, D. D., New Haven, Ct.
Bailey, Benjamin, M. D., New York.
Ball, Hon. Gideon J., Erie, Pa.
Barefoot, Isaac, Brantford, Ont., Can.
Ballard, Horatio, Homer.
Barker, Hon. George, Fredonia.
Barker, Peter, East Evans.
Barry, Rev. Wm., Chicago, Ill.
Barry,Maj.Gen.Wm.F.,Washington,D.C.
*Bates, Edward, St. Louis, Mo.
Baugher, J. F., Reading, Pa.
*Beers, Seth, Litchfield, Ct.
Bennett, Henry D., Ann Arbor, Mich.
Bennett, Joseph, Evans, N. Y.
Biddle, Hon. Horace P., Logansport, Ind.
Bigelow, George, Sardinia.
Billings, Walter P., St. Louis, Mo.
Bishop, Albert W., Little Rock, Ark.
Blake, F. N.,U. S.Consul, Hamilton,Can.
Blettner, Rev. John, Sault St. Mary,Mich.
Bliss, Jno. H., Erie, Pa.
Boyd, Prof. Erasmus J., Monroe, Mich.
Bradish, Prof. Alvah, Fredonia.
Brevoort, J. Carson, Brooklyn.
Bristol, C. C., Manchester, N. J.
Brown, S. G., Pres. Hamilton Coll., N. Y.

Brown, Simon, Concord, Mass.
Bailey, George, Hartford, Ct.
Bull, Wm. H., Bath.
Burch, Isaac H., Chicago, Ill.
Burrows, Hon. Lorenzo, Albion.
Bush, Hon. John T., Clifton, Ontario.
Bushnell, Charles I., New York.
Butler, Thomas B., Norwalk, Ct.
Calkins, W. A., Colden.
Cameron, Hon. Hugh, La Crosse, Wis.
Campbell, Wm. W., Cherry Valley.
Cary, V. R., Boston, N. Y.
Caton, Hon. John D., Ottawa, Ill.
Caulkins, Miss F. M., New London, Ct.
Chamberlain, Hon. Mellen, Boston,Mass.
Chapman, Rev. F. W., Rocky Hill, Ct.
Charlton, Hon. B. E.,Hamilton,Ont.,Can.
Charlton, John, Lynedoch, Ont., Can.
Cheney,T. Apoleon, LL. D., Havana,N.Y.
Cherry, Hamilton, Tonawanda.
Chester, Prof. Albert H., Hamilton Coll.
Chester, Augustin, Washington, D. C.
Chester, Rev. Chas. H., Havana, N. Y.
Chester,Col.JosephLemuel,London,Eng.
Child, George W., Philadelphia.
Clark, John, Lancaster, N. Y.
*Clark, Joshua, V. R., Manlius.
*Colegrove, Bela H., M.D., Sardinia,N.Y.
Collins, Hon. Isaac C., Cincinnati, O.
Cooke, Josiah P., Jr.,Cambridge, Mass.
Cooley, Hon. Thos M., Ann Arbor,Mich.
*Cornell, Hon. Ezra, Ithaca.
Cowley, Charles, Lowell, Mass.

* Deceased.

29

Craig, Isaac, Allegheny City, Pa.
Crandall, Hon. Hiram, Syracuse.
Cruickshank, Ernest A., Fort Erie, Ont.
Danforth, Elliott, Scoharie Co.
Darby, John F., St. Louis, Mo.
Dart, Hon. Wm. A., Potsdam.
Davies, Hon. Henry E., New York.
Davis, Dr. Chas. H. S., Meriden, Ct.
Dean, George W., Washington, D. C.
Dennis, Charles, Jr., Brooklyn.
De Peyster, Gen. J. Watts, Tivoli, N. Y.
Dewey, Abner, Evans, N. Y.
Diven, A. S., Elmira.
Dodd, Hon. Edward, Argyle.
Doolittle, Hon. James R., Racine, Wis.
*Doty, Lockwood L., Albany.
*Drake, Samuel G., Boston, Mass.
Draper, Lyman C., Madison, Wis.
Driggs, Urial, Tonawanda.
Durrie, Daniel S., Madison, Wis.
Dutcher, Luther L., St. Albans, Vt.
Eliot, W. G., St. Louis, Mo.
Ely, Hon. E. Selden, Cheektowaga.
Emmons, Dr. C., Concord.
Erwin, Charles H., Painted Post.
Evans, Prof. Ellicott, Clinton.
Ewell, Dexter, Alden.
Ewell, Joseph E., Alden.
Fargo, Wm. C., Syracuse.
*Fellows, Joseph, Bath.
Fenton, Hon. R. E., Jamestown.
Flagler, Thomas T., Lockport.
Fleming, Robert E., Fort Wayne, Ind.
Flint, Austin, M. D., New York.
Follett, Oran, Sandusky, O.
Foote, Elial T., New Haven, Ct.
Force, Gen. M. F., Cincinnati, O.
Fosdick, Morris, Springville.
Foster, Harrison T., Marilla.
Foster, John, Chicago, Ill.
Fox, Hon. Benjamin, Springfield, Ill.
Fox, Hon. E. Williams, St. Louis, Mo.
Frank Augustus, Warsaw.
Freeman, Dr. Samuel, Saratoga Springs.
Frothingham, W., Albany.
Gates, Henry K., New York.
Geddes, George, Camillus.
Gilman, D. C., New Haven, Ct.
Gleason, Alfred W., Toledo, O.
Glowacki, Henry J., Batavia.
Godfrey, E. W., North Collins.
*Goodman, A. T., Cleveland, O.
Gordon, George Wm., Boston, Mass.
Gould, Prof. B. A., Cambridge, Mass.
*Granger, Francis, Canandaigua.
Gray, Prof. Asa, LL. D., Cambridge, Mass.
Gray, Dr. John P., Utica.
Greenwood, Isaac J., New York.

Hale, A., Minneapolis, Minn.
Hall, Edwin, D. D., Auburn.
Hall, Hon. S. H. P., Binghamton.
Hamilton, Dr. Frank H., New York.
Hardin, Gen. M. D., Chicago, Ill.
Harwood, R. Adm'l A.A., U.S.N., Wash'n.
Havens, A., Wales.
Hawkins, H. H., Silver Creek.
Hilgard, J. E., Washington, D. C.
Hill, Dr. Edgar C., Lewiston.
Hitchcock, A., Cheektowaga.
Hoadly, Charles J., Hartford, Ct.
Hodge, Lorin, Jefferson, O.
Holley, George W., Niagara Falls.
Hollister, Gideon N., Litchfield, Ct.
Hopkins, T. A., Amherst.
Horsford, Prof. E. N., Cambridge, Mass.
Hosmer, James K., Deerfield, Mass.
Hosmer, Wm. H. C., Avon.
*Hotchkiss, Wm., Lewiston.
Hough, Franklin B., Lowville.
Hough, Prof. G. W., Albany.
Houghton, George F., St. Albans, Vt.
Hudson, Hon. C., Lexington, Mass.
Huidekoper, Alfred, Meadville, Pa.
Hunt, G. B., Clarence.
Hunt, T. Sterry, LL. D., Boston, Mass.
Huntington, Edward, Rome.
Hurd, C. W., Elma.
Irish, Ira E., East Evans.
Irvine, Wm. A., Irvine, Pa.
Jackman, W., Youngstown.
James, F. H., Lancaster.
James, John H., Urbana, O.
Jarvis, Edward, Dorchester, Mass.
Johnson, Crisfield, East Aurora.
Johnson, Sir Wm., Montreal, Can.
Jones, Morven M., Utica.
Jones, Wm. P., Portsmouth, N. H.
Judson, ——, Brant.
Kellogg, A. Otis, M. D., Utica.
*Kelly, Wm., Rhinebeck.
Kendrick, Prof. A. C., D. D., Rochester.
Kennedy, J. C. G., Washington, D. C.
*Kerr, J. W. Simcoe, Well. Sq., Ont., Can.
King, Dr. David, Newport, R. I.
King, Hon. H., Washington, D. C.
Kingman, Eliab, Washington, D. C.
Kirtland, J. P., Cleveland, O.
*Kite, Nathan, Philadelphia.
Lake, Hon. Delos, San Francisco, Cal.
Lathrop, Paul B., Elma.
*Leake, Isaac Q., Jackson, Mich.
*Lee, Prof. Chas. A., M. D., Peekskill.
Lee, Col. J. E., Washington, D. C.
Leech, Hiram P., Washington, D. C.
Lewis, Geo. W., Fredonia.
Lewis, Maj. J. R., U. S. A., Atlanta, Ga.

* Deceased.

*Lewis, Winslow, M. D., Boston, Mass.
Loomis, Prof. Elias, LL. D., N. Haven, Ct.
Lossing, Prof. Benson J., Dover Plains.
Love, John L., San Francisco, Cal.
Lovering, Prof. J., Cambridge, Mass.
*Luckey, Rev. Samuel, Rochester.
Lyman, Benjamin, Montreal, Can.
Lyman, Prof. C. S., New Haven, Ct.
Maltby, Benjamin, Colden.
Margry, Pierre, Paris, France.
Marvin, Hon. Richard P., Jamestown.
Marvin, Selden E., Albany.
McBeth, Dr. J., Wales.
McMaster, Guy H., Bath.
McMillan, J. H., Collins.
Merriam, Hon. C. L., Locust Grove.
Merritt, J. P., St. Catharines, Ont.
Minard, John S., Cold Creek.
Mix, David E. E., Batavia.
Moore, E. M., Rochester.
Moore, Geo. H., LL. D., New York.
Morgan, Hon. E. B., Aurora, Cayuga Co.
Morgan, Hon. Edwin D., New York.
Morgan, Lewis H., Rochester.
*Moulton, Joseph W., Roslyn.
Mullin, Joseph, Watertown.
Munsell, Joel, Albany.
Murphy, Henry C., Brooklyn.
Myer, Gen. A. J., Washington, D. C.
*Mygatt, Henry R., Oxford.
Nason, Rev. E., Billerica Mills, Mass.
Neff, L., West Seneca.
Newberry, Prof. J. S., Columbia College.
Nice, John, Grand Island.
Niven, A. C., Monticello.
*Norton, Hon. Edw., San Francisco,Cal.
O'Callaghan, E. B., Albany.
Olmstead, Rev. I. G., Fort Edward.
O'Reilly, Henry, New York.
Orr, Alvin, Holland.
Otis, Calvin N., Cuba.
Parker, A. J., Albany.
Parker, N. H., Versailles.
Parkman, Francis, Boston, Mass.
Peacock, Wm., Mayville.
Pearson, Prof. J., Union College.
Perkins, Prof. G. R., Utica.
*Person, Chas. P., Aurora, Erie Co.
Peters, Theodore C., New York.
Phelps, E. J., Burlington, Vt.
Phelps, J. A., Titusville, Pa.
Phinney, Elihu, Cooperstown.
*Phinney, H. F., Cooperstown.
*Pierce, M. B., Versailles.
Pierrepont,Hon.W.C.,Pierrepont Manor.
Plumb, Rev. A. H., Chelsea, Mass.
Pool, Fitch, Danvers, Mass.
Porter, A. A., Niagara Falls.

Porter, A. H., Niagara Falls.
*Porter, A. S., Niagara Falls.
*Porter, P. B., Niagara Falls.
Potter, A., East Hamburg.
Pratt, Elon G., St. Louis, Mo.
Pratt, Lyman, Eden.
Pratt, Zadock, Prattsville.
Prentice, Hon. A. W., Norwich, Ct.
Pruyn, Hon. J. V. L., Albany.
Putnam, Douglas, Marietta, O.
Randall, H. S., Cortland Village.
Ransom, Col. H. B., Clarence.
Read, Hon. J. M., U. S. Min. to Greece.
Redfield, Heman J., Batavia.
*Reed, Charles M., Erie, Pa.
*Rich, C. B., Newstead.
Rich, Thomas G., Stamford, Ct.
Riley, Aaron, Aurora, Erie Co.
Riley, P. D., Holland.
Safford, Prof. J. M., Nashville, Tenn.
Sandford, Laura G., Erie, Pa.
Saxton, Gen. Rufus, U. S. Army.
Seaman, E. C., Ann Arbor, Mich.
Searls, S. W., Wales.
Severance, C. C., Concord.
Sewall, E. Quincy, Watertown.
Sheldon, Henry L., Middlebury, Vt.
Shepard, C. O., U.S. Consul, Leeds, Eng.
Sherman, D., Forestville.
Sherman, John, North Collins.
Shipman, A. B., Syracuse.
Shipman, Wm. D., Hartford, Ct.
Silliman, Prof. B., New Haven, Ct.
Simmons, C. C., St. Louis, Mo.
Simms, J. R., Fort Plain.
Simpson, Gen. J. H., Washington, D. C.
*Skinner, J. B., 2d, Attica.
*Skinner, St. John,B. L.,Washing'n, D.C.
Slafter, Rev. E. F., Boston, Mass.
Smalley, David A., Burlington, Vt.
Smith, Cephas, East Hamburg.
Smith, George, Upper Darby.
*Smith, Junius A., Batavia.
Soper, H. U., Batavia.
Southwick, Edmund, Evans.
Southwick, Enos, Collins.
Southwick, Job, Brant.
Southwick, Josiah, Evans.
Spaulding, L. A., Lockport.
*Spencer, Platt B., Geneva, O.
*Stanley, John M., Detroit, Mich.
Stannard, Capt. B. A., Cleveland, O.
Stanton, Wm., Brant.
Starkey, Rev. O. F., Niagara Falls.
Starr, George W., Erie, Pa.
*Stevens, A. S., Attica.
Stevenson, Moses, Versailles, N. Y.
St. John, O. S., Willoughby, O.

* Deceased.

Stone, Wm. L., Saratoga Springs.
Storrs, Wm. C., Rochester.
Street, A. B., Albany.
*Strong, Nathaniel T., Irving.
Taylor, Col. R. M., Washington, D. C.
Thompson, Rev. M.L.R.P.,Cincinnati,O.
Tillman, Prof. S. D., New York.
Titus, J. M., New York.
Trask, Wm. B., Boston, Mass.
Treat, Judge Samuel, St. Louis, Mo.
Trott, James F., Niagara Falls.
Trowbridge, Thos. R., New Haven, Ct.
Trumbull, J. Hammond, Hartford, Ct.
*Tryon, A. S., Lewiston.
Turner, N. A., East Aurora.
Tyson, Philip R., Baltimore, Md.
*Upham, C. W., Salem, Mass.
Van Campen, George H., Olean.
Van Cleve, James, Lewiston.
Van Pelt, Wm., M. D., Amherst.
Van Rensselaer, Gen. B. F., Albany.
Van Schaack, H. C., Manlius.
Van Tassel, T., Salina.
Vinton, Rev. J. A., D. D., Boston, Mass.
Wadsworth, James, New York.
*Wadsworth, James S., Geneseo.
Waite, John T., Norwich, Ct.
Waldo, Rev. M., Hornellsville.
Walker, Edward C., Detroit, Mich.
Walker, Prof. Chas. R., Detroit, Mich.
Walker, Rev. J. B. R., Hartford, Ct.

Wallbridge, T. C., Belleville, Ont.
*Walworth, R. Hyde, Saratoga Springs.
Warren, O., Clarence.
Washington, P. S., Washington, D. C.
Weed, Monroe, Wyoming.
Wells, H., Aurora, Cayuga Co.
Wendell, George, Mackinac, Mich.
Wentworth, John, Chicago, Ill.
West, Prof. Charles E., Brooklyn.
White, Henry, New Haven, Ct.
Whitehead, A. P., Newark, N. J.
Whiting, Wm., Boston, Mass.
Whittlesey, Col. C., Cleveland, O.
Wilkeson, Samuel, New York.
Williams, J. B., Ithaca.
Williamson, Joseph, Belfast, Me.
*Willis, Wm., LL. D., Portland, Me.
*Wilson, Dr. Peter, Versailles.
Wiltse, L. G., Clarence.
Winchell, Prof. A., Ann Arbor, Mich.
Winchester, Prof. H., Reading Pa.
Wing, H. R., Glen's Falls.
Wood, Lyman, Wales Centre.
Woodruff, Maj. Israel C.,Washing'n,D.C.
Woolworth, Samuel B., Albany.
Worthen, Prof. A. H., Springfield, Ill.
*Wright, Rev. Asher P., Versailles.
Wright, Judge E., Boston, Mass.
Young, J. B., Amherst.
Younglove, T. M., Hammondsport.

HONORARY MEMBERS.

Bancroft, George, Washington, D. C.
Barnard, F. A. P., Pres. Columbia Coll.
*Buckingham, Wm. A., Norwich, Ct.
*Cass, Lewis, Detroit, Mich.
Davis, Noah, New York.
*Dickinson, Daniel S., Binghamton.
Dix, John A., New York.
*Everett, Edward, Boston, Mass.
Fish, Hamilton, Washington, D. C.
*Fisher, Samuel W., Clinton.
Hall, Hiland, N. Bennington, Vt.
Hall, Wm., Sr., Cleveland, O.
Hamlin, H., Washington, D. C.
Hawley, Joseph R., Hartford, Ct.
Hopkins, Mark, Northampton, Mass.
Jouett, St. Com'r Jas., Williamston, Mass.
*King, Charles, LL. D., New York.
*King, John A., Jamaica.

Lea, Isaac, LL. D., Philadelphia.
McMaster, James, London, England.
*Nelson, Samuel, Washington, D. C.
*Peabody, George, London, Eng.
Ruggles, Samuel B., New York.
*Scott, Lt. Gen. Winfield, New York.
*Seward, Wm. H., Auburn.
Seymour, Horatio, Utica.
*Storrs, Lucius, Cortland Village.
Swift, Gen., Brooklyn.
Washburn, E. B., U. S. Min., Paris, Fr.
Washburn, Emory, Cambridge, Mass.
Wetherell, Benj. F. H., Detroit, Mich.
Wilder, Marshall P., Boston, Mass.
Williams, G. P., LL.D., Ann Arbor, Mich.
Winthrop, Robt. C., Boston, Mass.
*Wool, Gen. John E., Troy.

* Deceased.

INDEX.